AFRICAN WRITERS S

221

The Graveyard Also Has Teeth

THE GRAVEYARD ALSO HAS TEETH

with

Concerto For An Exile

POEMS

SYL CHENEY-COKER

LONDON
HEINEMANN
IBADAN NAIROBI

Heinemann Educational Books Ltd
22 Bedford Square, London WC1B 3HH
P.M.B. 5205, Ibadan · P.O. Box 45314, Nairobi

EDINBURGH MELBOURNE AUCKLAND
HONG KONG SINGAPORE KUALA LUMPUR NEW DELHI
KINGSTON PORT OF SPAIN

Heinemann Educational Books Inc.
4 Front Street, Exeter, New Hampshire 03833, U.S.A

ISBN 0 435 90221 0

Set in Souvenir by GMGraphics, Harrow-on-the-Hill, Middlesex.
Printed in Great Britain by Fakenham Press Limited, Fakenham, Norfolk.

CONTENTS

THE GRAVEYARD ALSO HAS TEETH

Part I POEMS IN CONVERSATION WITH SIERRA LEONE

Part II POEMS IN CONVERSATION WITH DEATH

Concerto For An Exile

PREFACE

Venomous songs! Venomous love!

There is no sweeter song to death than the perfect concerto for
  love
A gypsy woman's flamenco sang in my soul!

But song by itself is no fertile language for death

Words?

Words too can be sacrilegious. I learnt that from Christ at Calvary
  The souls he has dismembered!

Wishing to explain my death, this terrain stinking of my filth
  walk on it if you dare you stand to lose your head!

It takes the savage language of a kick
to cure the heart of its persistent follies
That is, there is a beautiful splendour about violence
A violence the word has coloured with too much muck
and then?

Passion!

A force contemptuous of reason.

The nightingale sings of his sorrow
the moon his lover in her tipsiness demands and end to the dirge
but then to misquote Zweig, to judge a soul carried away by
  passion
would be as ridiculous as to call a storm to account or to bring
a lawsuit against a volcano

my omnivorous heart? If you entered it yesterday

you would have died of the muck the world deposited there!

Ah! but it's closed to all smiles.

Why?
The tree of agony wickedly planted in my soul!

It has three branches but I refuse to tell
what they are because I stand innocent of my death!

Ah! what stubborn head (especially mine) has ever resisted
the treachery of love? A love with too many holes
is no savoury dish. My proof?

The pine-needles in my eyes. That taste of love;
it is too bitter, too bitter I say!

Ah walk on my terrain if you dare
you stand to lose your head and your soul too!

Warning to all innocent hearts
failing which you stand to be deceived!

THE TRAVELLER

For Tchicaya U Tam'si

I limp with you on every road of your passion
Creole and Congolese regiments of the dead
I seek not my tomorrow my heart weighs me down
I bleed with carcinoma in my soul
I plunder my head with joy and kill the millepedes of my race
the blood upon my hands is nothing but the rotten phlegm from
   my nose

the philanthropists the beautiful assassins
the miserable blacks wanted a new race
despite the warnings in meteors of blazing sun
that planting metamorphous souls
inside the obedient belly of the soil was germicidal rot
the sea awaited the expedition the sea awaited the negroes
and hungrily swallowed them for delight the sea swallowed the
   stars
the moon in agony with the filth spat at the desolate voyagers
and warned that such outrage could provoke the nemesis of the
   sea

papaloas of the plantations
they raped the flora and fauna of the land
the birds danced in orgy with the voyagers the birds danced with
   the stars
I got my disgrace from that first rape
so tragic was it that the world had a radioactive fit

O my Portuguese conquistador
do not speak to me about my genealogy
a slaver's knife chewed my umbilical cord
twenty-five drops of my blood Pedro da Cinta
1462 means nothing to me the sea to rock the belly

was I captain of the ship William Wilberforce
what monument shall I build to you inside my soul

then that soul my heart my soul of iron and nails!
which one was weak enough to permit this bleeding in my life
my soul too open too trusting to resist the treachery of love –
having known love I lost my soul in the flames

thorns too visible in my smile I come to Quebec
trying to forget that Argentine bird who fled with my soul
that senorita fled with my soul on her chariot of flames Lady
    Medea
listen I groan with Jason loving her in my wounds
my anguish equals his, chorus of Corinths
Zeus your Medea my virago my ruthless Cristina!
I longed to carve my child upon that woman's womb . . .
oh I write a poem in solitude with the night

solitude my destiny stay solitude stay
for tonight happiness might make love to me
and I shall forget the tree of agony planted in my soul
that tree with branches of gervas upon which my Argentine bird
    laughs!

6

HYDROPATHY

Go on laugh
at my ancestry
which put the sickness
in my head beautiful
like the sea
which vomited me out!

I think of Sierra Leone
and my madness torments me
all my strange traditions
the plantation blood in my veins
my foul genealogy!
I laugh at this Creole ancestry
which gave me my negralized head
all my polluted streams
not one river shedding its pain
to cleanse me behind this bush of thorns
then seeing me clean scars off my back
or this lewd head hydropathy and soiled
not screaming in delirium about my rape

one summer's rape gave me life
the sperm in the grass stinks of my filth
behind that grass fiery with occult
three women of neurotic sex
splashing their cunts with the licentious blood
of female copperheads pissed on my soul
all my body transformed into oxidized death
it was seen in the swelling of my head
that my flesh will be carrion for the jackals
when they dance behind the bush of armoured thorns
they dance to our mourning there in Freetown
I dance with them here in exile

feet deep in my heart
all my limbs thrust against the acid wind
if blade will sharpen that wind
imagine my alcoholic head at dance
but from what plantation
and from what people my rum
in my country the Creoles drink only
Black and White with long sorrows
hanging from their colonial faces!

THE CRUCIFIED

Deserted and betrayed
my heart beats heavy in its pain
it feels the love which weighs
it down. Love, sweet, bitter
passion, hot as the Chinese revolution!

The night is foul its equinox my bitter days
the hounds baying at the moon have less rage than the hurricane
   in my heart
to see the hounds at bark the night knows the fire preparing my
   deaths
O night, O planet, my miserable horizon!

now I die now I live the cyclical sadness
groaning by a river where I drop my pus of death
to live in harmony with my dead voyagers
my deaths will be slow, the assassins be rewarded
what faggots they will burn upon my flesh
so that I shall learn in suffering, so that I shall learn in dying
that love by the heart and the flesh makes the embers in my eyes

the love which bleeds from the heart is the purest of all
laughed a woman in my life! the winter my nightmare laughed
   with her

reading Borges and Neruda
I torture myself the knife from an Argentine's hand
and sometime last winter waiting for love in vain
I killed the phallus in me
thus I wish to live the obedient eunuch
loving only those who set fire to my flesh

the fire in the well my eyes is it by you
that I have the nightmares in my sleep

the nightmares which winnow the sleep from my eyes
sending me into the world of those who sleep with heads upside
   down
the strange sleep of the centaurs because in life, life transformed
   them
into demons, because in death death transformed them into
   dragons:
my monstrous voyagers!

ah I have the nightmares in my sleep
the storms which make the tremors in my sleep
night my derision, night my florescence
are these all there are to it
these dead flowers in my soul
or this desire festooning my head with three devices
sewn by the amazon who comes to me brandishing the flame
she puts on my soul?

certain visions have been seen
there is too much agony in me to want to live tomorow
there is my river flowing with blood
also what do I have to offer but my nose
which makes the phlegm filth of Sierra Leone
the stench of politics and love is lascivious in my belly

Oh! nail me to my cross, the two thieves also, I am they
my three deaths, one for myself, one for my people, and one for
   Sierra Leone
and to you my brothers while you watch these deaths
prepare to burn your degrees and other academic shit
tomorrow will be rough armed with peasants' teeth
I have seen it, poet in agony four years mad
walk away from this my bitter terrain down to the path the sea
and drink the mad gush of my blood!

ANALYSIS

I am in my room observing my record player covered with dust
my mountainous library from Brecht to Zola
Pushkin is absent killed in a duel for love
as they die everywhere poets without honour
across the hall Mike snores ferociously
because the landlady let him sleep without his rent
outside the summer smothers the day

the humidity of the summer pissed through the leaves
of every tree . . . if I dodge the heat tell me which lake
to cool my rage? lying to your shadow by day the shadow
knows your bright ugliness by night! ah taste the vinegar
in the air it has more sweetness than my joy

my rage my tears, my groaning, my raving
to whom? for whom? to whom I ask?

to Africa for permitting a perpetual butchery of her womb
to those who barter her on Wall Street and the World market
muckrakers, smugglers, politicians and the like
to know them by their smiles Wall Street buys your heart!
think of your agony Africa your capitalist war-mongers
those long queues your children straddled strapped to your backs
waiting for those who rule who lead you into the makets of slavery
do they sell you for the rand or for the dollar?

to America whose pulse beats too loudly in my heart
your hands your lips your love too vicious to poets
your ladies with false eyelashes who kill your poets
America think of your involvements
those who died with napalm in their eyes
were they necessary for your salvation or for your balance of
    payments?

Cuba is alive in spite of your insane blockade
the Vietnamese shoot through the eyes although you control the
   sky
I am no water fountain the mucus you have poisoned in my head
I die from breathing your air your love is a machine in my heart
but I must think of Africa which is obedient to your dollar

there after you have seen the filth
those who dance under the chandeliers
while others coax the stubborn fires in the huts
you learn that at the price of sanity
you walk with one eye open and the other one shut!

MONOLOGUE

Every dog asleep!

I move my bed across the room
waiting to catch the night in its flight

my alcoholic head revealing my crimes
the mucus comes gushing out soiling the arms soiling the soil

every hour of these nights torments me
the lions roaring in my head leading
the tessitura for everyday I live in my rage

then it's no longer these vertical nights
which frighten me but my life the existential emptiness!

paint my horizon black
hammer my head with a volley of slugs

give my voyagers the stink of rotten cadavers
and my heart a continental kick!

then how soon this death I plead for every night?

it is better that I be gone now
I will surely suffer for my crimes
and my outrageous kindness also

I have insulted the world with my ubiquitous humanism
I have kindled the drab oriflamme of ancient religiosity
who blames them then for delivering me to my fate?

I say paint my horizon black
put a pangolin inside my belly
let it eat there the bread of deliverance
so that I'll be saved from
this sour passover that warms my bloated throat

I have enjoyed a sumptuous feast
cooked with the blood of my Creole ancestors!

TOILERS

These soothing words
for all lazy minds
like the clock at noon
its hands dulled
by improper automation.
Every minute a tumour
of a volcano poised
at the heart of
a continent – Africa!

a claustrophobia in my room because the sun is in orgasm there!

then the dawn then the sickle the axe to smite me
because the sun has ejaculated the bad sperm of the drought

this drought which is no sieve in my hands
a farmer his wife shift the soil shift the sperm
the bad sperm of the century curling in their hands the seed the
    promise
with eyes of iguana with head of hippo disappears in the earth
to come to life in that woman's womb bursting in flames the
    savage birth
splitting her belly because the woman had waited too long for the
    dead foetus
to cry in that stubborn earth denying her her rest

then those who came to watch died from the shock
those who came to mourn died from perdition
those who came in the ambulance forget their official cards
O woman O sorrow our horrible bureaucracy!

now the farmer his night following the stupid guidance of the stars
with their own laziness smelling of alcohol because the world
    demands
that they be drunk at all times this tyrannical rule from year to year
showed the farmer his labour the grass hut his agony

14

his head on the stone bed of his grief
cruelly the night brings the farmer his child
the bad sperm of the century running through his veins
made him lewd poisoning his belly the putrid soil of his belly
his skin is peeling off his dog-starved bones
and the farmer has fallen asleep vomiting a blond saliva
farmer there are so many stupid heads
in your dreams gloating with the thirst
for black opulence much too afraid to share the sacrifice with you

but I am no peasant farmer my name is government
and I work in an air-conditioned office with ten telephones
my days are limpid with brandy and ginger
cruising slovenly at noon to my villa in the restricted zone
proudly overlooking the sea
and my dogs keep you off my luxuriant lawn
inherited from the colonial master
and my children are locked up in super elitist schools
thus prohibiting the contagion of your diseases

yesterday it was independence celebration
and we threw in July fourteen as added attraction
because ex-British or ex-French we have to pay our obedience
howling the logistics about which was best colonial or ourselves
forgetting you my source that I made so black

now shamelessly I dare to mourn with you
with crocodile tears on paper nonsensical to you
infuriating your heart

farmer I arm myself with my lies
predicting your carnage
I am no fool I know you demand my skull!
but my peasant my sins are too visible and at the end of your
    uprising
dangle my head on your sword the fraternal oppressor!

FREETOWN

Africa I have long been away from you
wandering like a Fulani cow
but every night
amidst the horrors of highway deaths
and the menace of neon-eyed gods
I feel the warmth of your arms
centrifugal mother reaching out to your sons
we with our differnt designs innumerable facets
but all calling you mother womb of the earth
liking your image but hating our differences
because we have become the shame of your race
and now on this third anniversary of my flight
my heart becomes a citadel of disgust
and I am unable to write the poem of your life

my creation haunts me behind the mythical dream
my river dammed by the poisonous weeds in its bed
and I think of my brothers with 'black skin and white masks'
(I myself am one *heh heh heh*)
my sisters who plaster their skins with the white cosmetics
to look whiter than the snows of Europe
but listen to the sufferings of our hearts

there are those who when they come to plead
say make us Black Englishmen decorated Afro-Saxons
Creole masters leading native races
but we wandering African urchins
who will return one day
say oh listen Africa
the tomtoms of the revolution
beat in our hearts at night

make us the seven hundred parts of your race
stretching from the east to the west
but united inside your womb
because I have dreamt in the shadows of Freetown
crashing under the yoke of its ferocious civilization!

ABSURDITY

All my people
would die if
you split open my belly!

You do not know how it feels
to be the rot of your country
even the vultures
will be afraid of your corpse

my mother you have given me
a perennial prison
and I carry the keys around
as I am my own murderer
and blessed be the death I will die
it will reveal my horizon to me

there is no labour
greater than my agony
or this sorrow destroying my soul
here is my soul in fuel and flames
crinkling in my hands
I offer it to you
take the carcasses away
but don't kill that flame
that lights my people's eyes

I am the beginning the running image
and the foul progency of my race
these strange Afro-Saxon negroes
and for deceiving the world
about our absurdity
behold my negralized head in flames!

THE MASOCHIST

don't ask me
why I look so sad
I did not know my father
only an apparition
who said he was a phoenix
my face is the apocalypse
of my misery
mind and body examined
I stand a paradigm of sorrow

Creole Creole
one is the raped mulattress
who wets the slave bed
after the planter is spent

the nigger who does not know
his own genes who knows
his Afro-Saxon name
who does not know his own cross
who grins at the crucifixion
of his own sex

yesterday I remember
I had performed the lavabo
the lavabo which cleansed the stain
the white Creole madness!

MY SOUL O OASIS!

Trying to curtain
myself in the night
there comes the news
to shatter my heart –
my heart like my brothers
sick in the head!

They shot five soldiers dead last night
sorcerers of a counter-revolution
but to die in the inferno of Sierra Leone
does not equal my distress
which has the red flame of a violated soul

shadows of the conquistadors
I do not know, Pedro da Cinta
and the Argentine Pedro de Alvarado
and all the other djinns of Sierra Leone
which one of you plundered the tree of agony in my soul?
the guns echoed in Argentina

I loved dangerously without thinking of my years
my love is a poniard, see it tear at my heart
and give me a river crying of the spirits
so that upon its bank you will see me sad
singing of their gangrene

do they keep the fire and the sword
these men who dance passionately in the holocaust
if so will they bring back the soul
which fled from my life?

Borges in Buenos Aires writes me a poem
which is not the cure for his eyes
which is not the milk from my sweetheart's breasts
to mull the oasis of my distress
only the disembowelled belly of a youth
tells me the Sierra is in good health!

19

CONCERTO FOR AN EXILE

And the guns roared on
in Sierra Leone and Argentina
to plunder the tree of agony
in my soul!

The news of the coups the bullets in my soul!
I plunge into the streets holding the dead in my head
I deface my face with my leprous hands
I flee from a pack of hounds
tuned to the reverberations in my heart

what poem shall I write for my fratricidal brothers
whose lust has made the Sierra a volcano too bloody in my life
Brigadier Bangura General La Nusse my soul executioners
what revolutions shall I start for you
they who should join the revolution are dead decalcified body
    and soul
and I am stripped of my vanity my love my joy
my vanity for wishing to marry two continents in love
I know neither the days nor the nights of my days
the nights which cheat me standing headstrong upon my passion

away in Sierra Leone the boulevards of corpses
they shot them and slit their bellies for proof of their subversion
they were men of my salvation so they said who faced the eunuch
    Christ
lying upside down on that ravaged Sierra Leonean earth
and drunkenly talked about Che writing illogicalities for revolts
but in speaking of those revolutions a savage bird entered my soul
to sing me a concerto for pain my lady sang me a concerto of
    betrayal
that senorita's sex too sweet too vicious to my soul!

and I come to you once again Pedro da Cinta
my Portuguese conquistador my Sierra my volcano
was I a part of it the eruption tearing my country apart
I have my Nova Scotian madness my tree of agony
and let my brothers know I walk the streets of exile
clutching their bullets in my soul!

VOLCANO

First the innocent
next the guilty ones
next the makers of occult
then my brothers all demons
burnt in the fire-dance
beat out with gongs
on the conga-drum of my back!

And now this disquisition my Sierra!

was I a part of it
this gust of lava my pox
sordidly oozing into my skull
or Vesuvius madly phallic with rage
crippling the loins of men
somnolent and debauched

afterwards to sweeten their cannibal ecstasy
the lamias in their beds
voluptuous varanuses
insidiously slit open their aortas
thereby betraying their souls
O pedro O mountain
their disgusting apendages

thus seeing this pus at the mouth of a stream
brimming with their foam a stream like a prismatic bird
which at the long eclipse of the sun showed the world
that satyr teaming up with my voyagers
to rape the Sierra Leonean earth
I would drink the sap despoiling my blood

therefore I am raving and ranting
my rotten nose clogging up
my claws piercing my head

I no longer have a country centrifugal and proud
to assuage my long, miserable perdition
also the love which bludgeoned me
afflicted my head like a brain haemorrhage

and now the whirlwind night
lashing my grief right and left
my head at the flash of a whip spins on its neck
obeying the wind in its red madness
awkwardly following the path
my Portuguese conqueror
to you my phantom of steel I say to you

brand me deeper to nourish my bleeding heart!

STORM

Ah! the Sierra is a volcano

a gathering of clouds to announce
the coming storm the day lashes
at the trees its giddiness of rage

saluting the storm the storm prepares the day

I pass my hand over my brow
has it already the revolt of the times

the day grows mad and melancholy
the day turns blue with rancour
the day the seas flex their muscles
like giant anacondas
the day shows its fangs for the fools
to throw their heads there
alone a peasant sharpens his machete
to prepare himself for the storm
out of the corners of his drooping eyes
comes the octopus with its eight stiletto suckers
which must pass through the hearts of those
who live leisurely on the exchequer

they are heaving! see their gluttonous hearts
which neither blade nor storm has touched as yet
to reveal their rot that which they swallowed in haste

the bestiality of every regime
learnt from the bitter taste of the sun
languid with the ineptness of yesterday
but seen in the raging of the sea

they are failing to curtain the storm which prepares the day!

LOTUS-EATER

It is dawn mountain of madness I see your scorching hands!
see the day your corollary your sister seduce me
the jungle awake cataclysmal at heart
the panthers with eyes great charcoals of fire
and the mamba coiled waiting to strike
but tell me O mountain where are the hurricanes of the revolt
the revolution of the oppressed the revolt of the peasants
to make Africa less decrepit draining the blood of cowardice from
    veins
the murmurs in her belly what makes them so weak
gargantuan beast swallowing her black wretchedness!

when will it happen my Sierra
so that your torch may extirpate the sickness of agoraphobia
so that no ellipsoidal 'isms may bound your strength again
    that from
your belly may come the violent rays of a virginal sun so that my
thyroid gland may burst with the thundering of ten thousand
    tornadoes
that the voices of acacias the breaths of deserts the dams of rivers
the throats of savannahs the thighs of baobabs may cry REVOLT

on the slime bed of a beach a warthog pisses there
soothing the eyes soothing the souls of my voyagers
waterlily lovers waterlily excrescences
those to whom the sinking of ships the emptying of bowels
the crunching of the jaws of sharks are taken for joy
endlessly a storm rages on throws its hands around the necks of
    trees
bringing them down into the gulf of forewarning into the pits of
    oblivion
enjoying the storm a svelte mermaid combs her hair with a golden
    comb

her voice is the sweet flavouring of orchard-maple leaves
at the pull of the wind her tail pirouettes like a nude belly dancer
her eyes are the mocking gems of a sorceress' fire
her breast is the slime of a patch of quicksand
yet this wild heaving of my heart woman oh sorceress

throw a javelin there so that it keeps still!

ENVIRONNE

Head set round perfect
back humped heart and
claws mixed wickedly
in my perdition as I follow
The Road to Jamaica!

Losing my tracks one more time
I planted my feet deep in my heart
I followed the laxative shadows
emptying the bowels close to the river
which I must cross to get to my foul ancestors
a moonchild all demon danced before me
his body covered with thorn-warts
eye set centre on his face
laugh mirrors a grizzly bear
is he the preface to our holocaust
or these megrim attacks I nurse in my head
or perhaps my split memory of a woman
who offers her breast nude to the blade of wind
expecting a talisman for her teeth
likewise these shadows before me
all noxious all pestiferous in their blood of veratrum
which are sperms of death watering our deserts of madness
it would be nice to swallow their death-pox
should you refuse my pus of death
which I drop leisurely on this promenade
but for these vertebral forms lurking threateningly in the night
so colour your teeth with this sapodilla earth
to protect your ephemeral souls
this country is skeleton enough
without your wishing to die in it
bank to bank the river as they die
in the nights of the fire-dance
beat out with gongs on the conga-drum of my back!

PEASANTS

'The Masters of the Dew'
Jacques Roumain

The agony: I say their agony!

the agony of imagining their squalor but never knowing it
the agony of cramping them in roach infected shacks
the agony of treating them like chattel slaves
the agony of feeding them abstract theories they do not understand
the agony of their lugubrious eyes and bartered souls
the agony of giving them party cards but never party support
the agony of marshalling them on election day but never on
    banquet nights
the agony of giving them melliferous words but mildewed bread
the agony of their cooking hearths dampened with unuse
the agony of their naked feet on the hot burning tarmac
the agony of their children with projectile bellies
the agony of long miserable nights
the agony of their thatched houses with too many holes
the agony of erecting hotels but being barred from them
the agony of watching the cavalcade of limousines
the agony of grand state balls for God knows who
the agony of those who study meaningless 'isms in
    incomprehensible languages
the agony of intolerable fees for schools but with no jobs in sight
the agony of it all I say the agony of it all
but above all the damn agony of appealing to their patience
Africa beware! their patience is running out!

I THROW MYSELF TO THE CROCODILES

It is finished!

this sweet wagging of tongues
the strange bedfellows
Africa puts in my bed
the price of this deal dissects my groins

count your dirty rands my brothers
count them with your hands
sanguinary for gold
my brothers of dismemberment
detonating the dynamites in my soul

of late thinking about Africa
I have felt the pachyderms
charging at my heart:
I delight in their stampede!

I understand I understand
the rationality of it all
the A-B-C of the communist threat
this need to unite devil and saint under the banner of Christ
tell me what hyperdulia I'll make for Mary my virgin of saints

Christ will surely pay for it
this strange obedience to his will
those who consent to be hewers of woods
his black drawers of water brothers of my disembowelment
to be paid in strokes his bloody salvation

the riviera they are building
with goldfish in the lagoons
I shall be clown for the tourists

I'll throw myself to the crocodiles
their jaws will be less treacherous to me
gentler than the words of my brothers
who sell the peasants for the black gold of their wives

if they make a bed of thorns my joy
ah what burning grass they will swallow in death!

MISERY OF THE CONVERT

A protestant
I swore I would be chaste
to worship Mary the virgin of saints
my sex is a sterile seed in the wind
it has the sickness of my soul
Christ I have your vanity in my head
century to century summer to summer
ocean to ocean continent to continent
I carry the blessings of your rape
I was a king before they nailed you on the cross
converted I read ten lies in your silly commandments
to honour you my Christ
when you have deprived me of my race

I remember one night
dreaming in a missionary house
I had driven the shadows out
spitting at their tomtom Gods

I was sane
only when King George died
Sunday was a present for me
grandmother drooling in her room
beneath the shadow of King George
did not begrudge the treats
– one pair of shoes
– one pair of socks
– one pair of shorts
all in the name of the lord
I did not know to be a Creole and a saint
meant to have sung the ballad of your grief
when the saviour himself did not rejoice

*

Christ you must have been a peasant in your time
you died naked on your cross
it was the church that made you a landowner
and built you a catholic empire
tell me how many slaves you had
I have the asientos memorized in my head
how many burnt offerings do I owe
you my colour blind Christ
America eighty per cent white
sixty per cent black in your gas chambers

don't play on my susceptibility to pray
I have had enough of your forgiveness
I have not fared well against the army of your saints
give me time
four centuries are a long time to be drunk
with your passion my Christ
asking will somebody tell me my people's name
    *
but do you know my people's name
or where in this ocean they died
thrown off the slavers' ships
my people for whom I searched in vain

the moon led me I followed the sea
weed to weed my perdition beside me
no Portuguese flesh greeted me
not even a drop of sperm for my hair
yet I offered all my negritude
the water-soldiers played rattlesnakes round my legs
and I offered my soul offered all my negritude
to the sea waves the arms of a woman
the amazon to whom I offered my negritude
that senorita who tortured my heart
during my raw, pernicious winters in America

    *

I entered the sea
searched for the manifests of the trade
the waterdogs threatened my search
but ten souls came to me
each one stained with a different shit
God knows how many ships sailed this sea
emptying the slavers' shit
my own soul stained with the purest shit
I know it I was the first they branded in your name

Christ you definitely must have been a peasant in your time
I have drunk a cupful of your blood
cheaper than the blood of goats
costlier than the heads of my people
bodies without souls who hurl themselves
at the flames of your cross
the image of my perdition
      *
you have driven me mad
you have cast me in war against the army of your saints
a pagan now angered by the passion in your soul
I have deserted that soul
your torn borrowed soul
mine will await me fresh growth
on this lonely road which I walk
with my Creole head ablaze!

OBELISK

I have given up
trying to be a christian
in this nation of faggots
this country with its religious negroes
ugly in mourning for a eunuch Christ
O St Phillip if you only knew me
as a worthy disciple
you would have laughed at my insanity

I was myself the light in the dark
I branded Jesus on the chests of millions
but Christ you lied to me at Calvary
you did not die to save the world
but to make it a plantation where my people sweat

yet I was faithful I refused to become a communist
but the polluted rivers of my country have flooded
carrying away all my levitation
since then my despair
has grown taller than the obelisk of your cross
and I embrace no one Christ

here are my lamed penis
and my synclastic head of blood
they will stand for my credentials
although they torment me

I rejoice
for the idiosyncrasies of my brothers
I give my hands to your flames
I die to be posthumously rewarded
with an English grave with elephants dancing there!

SONG OF A ROCK

I am a rock
I am a mountain
I laugh with those
who laugh too loud

down in Freetown
they live haphazardly
discounting a holocaust
the vampires of sweet blood

I am a rock
I am a mountain
drinking with those
who drink too much

these meteors in my eyes
if they burn too fast
imagine the funeral train
of our final laughter!

LIFE

My body is aflame
I deliver my heart to the fire
the world which loves a sacrifice
eats my belly bit by bit these blazing entrails

a death in the afternoon
grown from the cancer in my soul
for the soul which tortures the flesh . . .
what head has a monopoly of slugs
more than my head

my body writhes in its pain
the djinns dance above me
the hemlock makes my soul soft
for the gall from a love-maiden's lips
see my traitors flock around me
to deliver me whom they inflamed

my body rots in the sun
my body poisons the flowers
ah the flowers die breathing my soul

I abandon my soul to the fire!

SHADOW

The day
pregnant with the sun
the night pregnant with the moon
have the shadows behind

my mother
was pregnant with my race
she carried a black seed
which blossomed
without the shadow of the race

my race a stream
listen a river without a source
it goes on this journey
that has no beginning
the end may be the beginning

a bleached man has nothing to lose
but the curse of his alientation!

AGONY OF THE DARK CHILD

I came to my mother
seeking the warmth of her breasts
she was frightened

you see I was dark
too dark my grandmother lamented

from the pharmacy
medicated bars of soap
drops of oil, drippings of water
and ornamented cures
for the naked body

she was frightened she told me
I was too dark!

MYOPIA

On rainy mornings
you will see them drenched
PEASANTS! shivering in their emaciated bones
along the boulevards of misery

the boulevards of this country
are railway tracks in my heart
a train of anguish runs on them
rage corollary of hunger
the ricepads of this country
are putrid marshlands in my soul
tended by no magic fertilizers

mountain if the wind blows tomorrow
make me a sabre of that wind
if the skeletons of stillborn promises
dry up in the catacombs
make me the incendiary bomb
if madness we must have
let me be the hangman hanging myself
hanging them hanging the day
not by its neck not by its belly
but by its heart seen in its great betrayal!

SOLITUDE

I am standing by a lake
watching the algae fondle with the swans
this purple heart within me I open my mouth
to sing the night the sad threnody of my life
my shadow my lake have you the solace I seek for the night

amidst the lake ten boats anchored lazily
bringing back my grief the memory of two hundred years
the passage bellowing inside me forcing my tears
oh Granville Sharp have you come to plague this bleeding heart
   again

my love my traitor
my callous aphrodite
I am no longer your Pushkin
I die no more for you
no sword in my hand
no duel in my heart
to guide me to my death coward between my legs

I save my tears for the swans
the night delivers me to my death
straight to the bar head in my rum
to drink my sorrows to the brink.

THE CANCER

Undoubtedly
there was a mistake at my birth
linking the constellations with the crab
but giving me no shell to protect myself
thus this clot of pus in my soul

don't ask me if I have loved
these pine-needles in my eyes
whose pain now reveals
a misogynous life
are the discerning flames
of my gangrenous heart

the superficiality of so many hearts
if they bring you love who is stupid enough
to kiss their hyena cheeks

then this world sickens me
with its fevent christianity
never a direct hearse
to the charnel-house

they are mad
to prepare a funeral for me
they will be guilty of blasphemy
invoking the name of their god
to deliver my pagan soul

after my death
I ask but one request
and only one

throw my body to the sharks!

NODAL

It is night
I suffer from fidelity
I lie awake in retrospect of last winter's groanings
my heart plays a game of darts
I cuddle my pillow in my heart
my tears betray my ingrained weakness
thus I suffer from fidelity

a falcon flays my memory with its wings
its wings are the eyelashes of this virginal moon
whose solar sperm makes a pond in my snout!
the wildebeests thrusting their horns into the grass of my heart

on the moon at night when its belly is red
let the serpent of fire devour my heart
O nightmare my guardian angel
I have sewn my love fetishes on my brow
the thread of wire knits a beautiful yoke there
and let the great bandanna of hell kindle itself in my eyes

and to this head which is the planed sissoo of a deceitful love
make upon it tattoos of a love farewell
and with the solen make at my cheeks scarifications
of an alphabeltical love O hurricane lover!
I have swallowed my roses red blue and hot dead in my soul
I have enjoyed my sunburnt kisses perched on my serrated lips
I have sweetened my rum with nitro-chloric acid *heh heh heh*
and for my solace let a pargurian dig into my skull!

I DIE BEFORE THIRTY

A skullful of rum!

a park my birthday no kisses no cake
no candles no flowers the night goes on

already I am old
without grey hair on my head
without mama or papa dead
without scion in my stream
no tomb earmarked for my rot

my beleaguered heart requiring a transplant
a dead man in my steps his shadow my own said
that which you seek is here
a paradise of peace
where neither pain nor love may cheat the soul in you
where the waters of purgatory may cleanse the poison in your
    heart
where the verisimilitudes of a few unknowns may open their paths
    to you

but behold the eunuch Christ!
resurrected by his own cunning
his uncrucified body and hands
falsifying his death his murderous disciples
St Phillip their leader my abandoned saint
dressed in cloaks of blood in cloaks of red
multiplied in number by all the other parasites of my flesh
burning my soul with the candles of damnation
my heart quivering smelling their enchanting feast
sweetly seducing me into the system of Dante's hell!

HOROSCOPE

The crab like the oasis
in my soul milky as the
moon which shelters the night
the crab sore as the scabs
on its back brilliant
as the night. . .
O Soul O Soul!

Why should I be living in the past
mesmerized by a love which nurtures
the incorrigible romantic in me
this breath of tomorrow fanning my ruptured soul
does little to release me from my pain

I do not sing for Rabearivelo imprisoned in himself
I do not sing for Baudelaire pathetic and debauched
nor for Tchicaya limping on his crutch
or for Rimbaud precocious and wild
no I do not sing for Verlaine head soaked in absinthe

I sing only for myself truly the paradigm of sorrow
all my sickness of head whirling at the whim of a wind
Creole ugliness of blue exrescences flushing at the
deaths of Sierra Leoneans all brothers of my misery

now moaning under my cross
I want my own calvary blazing in the sun
not the blue tranquillity of the clouds
or women with hyena cheeks wailing like hens
or men tearing at their hearts
no no no that won't do
let there be demons dancing at my death
I want my body pelted with stones
I want my nails ten inches long soaked in wasp poison
and for my eulogy let a faun sing me the song of a goat
but above all let there be dancing to relish my death!

IMPRISONMENT

And they flattened me
the violent storms in my belly
giant arms of riotous day
hot storms destructive
the sea their sister sings of its sorrow
made worse by my people
trapped between the sea-urchins
where the mermaids slug them
in the essence of their pain

what are they doing there
that they call me to their midst

I feel in my head the jolts of two thousand cyclones
let their force be my delirium

a shadow a memory the hands of a woman
I mean a woman pillorying my head
by loving that woman
nightmare sister of hurricanes
I am bleeding in this ghetto of agony!

ah! loving in the name of Christ
is that possible when he himself was a Judas
and those who betrayed me his vicious accomplices?

my sadness, my tears, my bitter taste of love!
where is the god of my refuge and strength
to thrown my body at him
I am no longer capable of love
I keep no more the faked commandments of Christ
I stand on the threshold of death
this death that follows love
offering my heart rotten as the garbage dump!

GUINEA

They have invaded Guinea
the Portuguese murderers
and their negro renegades
fascist enemies of the revolution
hurriedly dispatched by the NATO clique
exonerated by their papal asientos

they had hoped to enslave the peasants of Guinea
as they did four centuries ago
but oh the invincible armies of Alpha Yaya
down the mountains of Foutah Djallon
and my heart lights up
like a burning flame in the night

Bissau Bissau Bissau
I am of your image
in spite of my Creole absurdity
and six hundred Fulani negroes
behind the guilt of my country

I am not the renegade
who has forsaken your shores
I am not the vampire
gnawing at your heart
to feed capitalist banks
I am your poet
writing No to the world!

LICENTIOUS

Tell me O desert
do you know
my people's paths?

Stinking of a profligate's lust
I entered all the whorehouses in my path
entered all the brothels and harems
the moon shone in a nudist colony
as I slept with stately women
voluptuous and blasé
you should have seen me then
caricature of the chimera's king
I imagined myself king of satyrs
Adam betrayed by Eve
eating of the forbidden fruit
a bouquet of nosegays served as my bed
the twilight burned in my eyes
the ophiolater in his wild ecstasy

I am no cyclone O desert O oases
but what tree lacks my voodoo madness

sluggish movements of a demented beast
a man passes by a fire in his heart
where the hurricane uproots the trees
in its first madness which tells him
the desert's sand is soft
no match against the torrid storms of his quest
the oases groan in his heart
and to set the desert ablaze
the shrubs have let themselves be burnt

The Graveyard Also Has Teeth

PART I POEMS IN CONVERSATION WITH
SIERRA LEONE

Don't forget it, poet.
In whatever place or epoch
you make
or suffer History,
there'll always be,
lurking in ambush
the dangerous poem.

HERBERTO PADILLA
(Cuban poet)

ON BEING A POET IN SIERRA LEONE

A poet alone in my country
I am seeking the verisimilitudes in life
the fire of metaphors the venom of verse
my country you are my heart living like a devastated landscape
always the magic of being underground of burying truth
of shedding your metaphysical form
country I wish to die being your poet
I who have so condemned and sold you
I who have so loved and hated you
imagine my sadness, the poetry of being you
a colossus strangled by fratricidal parasites
have I betrayed you writing my hermetic poetry
I suffer the estrangement of being too 'intellectual'
at the university the professors talk about the poetry
of Syl Cheney-Coker condemning students
to read me in the English honours class
my country I do not want that!
do not want to be cloistered in books alone
I want to be the albatross learning and living your fits
I want only to plough your fields
to be the breakfast of the peasants who read
to help the fishermen bring in their catch
I want to be your national symbol of life
because my heart is heavy country and exile calls
beating the pangs of oblivion on my brow
I want once more like the common man
to love a woman without dying of love
to leave a son or daughter to remember my grave
country you my pain, my phoenix, my disastrous gloating python
in whose belly all my anger dies
I am going to be happy to stop carrying my pain
like a grenade in my heart, I want to be simple
if possible to live with you, and then one day die leaving
my poetry, an imperfect metaphor of life!

SONG FOR THE RAVAGED COUNTRY

Like an epilogue for the cadavers stretched alongside the truth
my song of anguish not learned from the blue nightingale
or these skeletons of plesiosaurian gods lingering in their eyes
like remoras sucking the foetus of their reactionary words
like caiman brilliant as poinsettia
like the belly revolting against the hunger fathering my cowardice
like a lance hurled from the obelisk of my rage
like pangolin gnawing at their bellies fattened with treachery
like aloes served with paprika producing the hiccups
like an aria cut from bamboo whirling in the oasis of my blood
like the cry of tornado at dawn echoing the jackals in heat
like my rage phallic with storm no oriflamme to drape
the violent pyres of my eyes that and the maddening currents
in my deep brow
like the lightning thunder of hooves which echoes the burst
in the ventricles the pulsating tusk of the narwhal
inside the drowned man's throat
my song floats reaching you my country skewered like goat
my song aria of serpent will float to your horns
not losing its fertile blood that it may grow like octopus
caressing the lines of their necks heaving forth their fall
the rain to drink to water these fields of our dreams
when I alone shall stand in the park sinking my poetry
between their teeth!

TALONS IN THE FLESH OF MY COUNTRY

But it does not matter that I live
in this country angry and sad
it does not matter that my words
reach only the 'privileged' ones
my words acid like the wounds bled
out of the times; the beasts' terror
momentarily plunders the human resilience
not guarded in their lair the beasts
slobbering these drought-infected waifs
I know, now that it does not matter
that my mouth trembles with my verse
seeing their treachery walking
arm-in-arm with justice the life howling
like a brochure of stamps and leones
the monolithic arrogance of power
they stuff themselves with for now!

    *

the nights are no longer safe
a mother cries inside a corridor
lit only by the moon's reflection
on that woman's torn taffeta
a hurricane passes inside her throat
outside her child with no eyes
but with a madman's laughter
dances to the hurricane
dreamer preparing the necromancy
the stinking cadavers wait for their mothers
but listen that woman has blood in her eyes without being drunk
that woman has lice in her blood without being sick
that woman has grey hair without being old
and naming her mother a shattered tomato
seeding the putrid vegetation
a thousand orphans without eyes
walk in this country mined with injustice

Lord the farce Lord the comedy!
robed in black and the sacred law books
the lizards lick over the buttered edges
swallowing the deadly contagion
and spit into the rivers the bile
where others little suspecting the lizards
drink of the precious waters
and I write about these beasts I write
these simple lines about these waters
I swim in the toxin in the waters
swallowing the tadpoles hatched in there
what have I not known in my land
the men of our dreams the men of our delusions
and Sierra Leone like a gargantuan beast
producing the slobber whose former image
I no longer remember because the cut-throats' wives'
teeth seen in the vulgar reflection of the sun
ape the talons tearing at the flesh of my country!

THE EXECUTED †

For Ibrahim Taqi and others

So that rebels and peasants when they are united
in my country no longer oppose me when I attack
the butchers in the thick of that revolt
giving me the sweat of the savannahs
at the eclipse of centrifugal blood
I drank from the dead displayed outside the prisons,
my priest is singing a song, not for these dead
my courageous dead, but for the living dead
and out of our regret the shrunken necks
bearing the marks of the dictator's hands
the crimes cooked in sorcery by their own priest
in the ubiquitous rape of the country

desires I understand so well, that they relish
better than their foul births
through which they arrived one morning
their souls in the service of mephistopheles
to prepare the coming of the gangrene
arming the gnats in the solar plexus of my people
at the beginning of their slow death

seeing clearly the canines of these desires
these oriflammes of their priest
will lure the innocents into their throats
for the feast of scurrilous fools
before the vertiginous collapse
of the lotus-eaters!
　　　*
they spread their bodies in the street
like dogs killed to pacify an implacable God
but to arm oneself with dead bodies
does not make the living crustaceans in the heart
thus they are sharpening their weapons, their cry of despair

to rise with the terrestrial suns
one day at the door of each widow
mourning the skeletons of her son

that day when their priest no longer destroys my soul
when I shall face them, my priest combating their priest
all my poetry will make my body slippery in their arms
living to tell the world how they have eaten the innocent
these cannibals in the absence of meats.

† This poem was first written in 1974 when they arrested Taqi
and others, in another version. The present version was written
after they were hanged.

THE SEA

Rise blood, phallus of malarial sea!
rise the coefficients of the storm
I chart my course on that savage storm
I am the coelacanth coming back the exhumation
of my bones when night rose with the gloating eloquence
of pythons!
and now denying all memory, the great putrefaction in Sierra
  Leone
I make my unctuous delirium I exit between the corals bearing
the shadow gambler in the equinoctial volcano of the sea!

I make a storm the just harvest of your designs
the fer-de-lance in the majesty of its eight feet
and the venomous onslaught of its love; thus the swell
of my muscle, the varicose of the woman mid-hour in the
  deliverance
of the storm; my pulse revolts against the ramparts of your fear
my obdurateness heightens this is the night
from what drunken fit do I greet you my Sierra Leone
woman torn from the flesh of my waters

I am Vesuvius the sixteenth I am Mauna Kea
my name is Mauna Loa behold the steaming calderas
of my lips! not a vessel in the calm of your eyes
has not known the heat oozed from the circular currents
of my body
and the blood squeezed from the sea-anemones
the crawling benthos multiplied in the icy pyramids
of my body leaps festooning you with the vertigos
of the tidal waves the murderous coefficients of my great depths!

HURRICANE AT NIGHT

I listen to the sea's lachrymose voice
echoes of the terrible dereliction
they give to my country
the men of Apollyon spreading the carnage
like the bandanna of victory for Christ
who knows all, the barbarian cosmology
of their politics read at the dance of djinns
amidst the rumours in the diabolical silence of the harmattan

monologues not stretching taut the throat
though my dead brother wears the crustaceous mask
of the sea's breath will make your revolt
the play of griffins in the succulent depths of their eyes

and the sea-horses parading like phalanges of despair
in the broad marrow of their phosphorescent face
prepare the volition of your tropical prick
when the sperm of your fiery protuberance
will make a hoe to toil the vegetable chest of my elan!

NAUSEA

Waking up this morning I live
just so that I can write on the pavement
with the blood of my country
just so that my heart will stretch
across this vast savannah to feel the other man's pain
on the hacienda in South America
I do not know his name Senor
but that Indian there brother of grief
and his mother who chews a thousand pieces of cocaine
to fill her stomach's void
I saw them once give a votive hand
to the peasants of this country
platitudinous and harsh

night and the city spreads its talons of fear!
I hear in the shanty a singing mulattress nursing her son
in whose eyes she reads the hungry patterns of death
wrought by those who have never sorrowed
by those who have never known pain
by those who have never died once
to die for their disgrace
I make them out slitting my throat
I smell them nights disguised as saints
ventricose for the mothers of gold
who offer their daughters
to be fucked on the surf of the sea
    *
they tell me they are mercenaries here
not a sister with cinnamon breasts
I remember them lachrymose heart
ventriloquists in the souls . . .!

they had not killed my brothers yet
they had not flattened my mother yet
nor given me this crop of thorns growing in my heart
daughters of the word on the flesh of the alphabet
minions of the politicians in the opulence of their necks!
the corruption in this country which nauseates me
to spit out my disgust and then die alive

remembering all these who denies me my death
laughing between the claws of vinegarroons

oh my land! my Sierra! my woman!
you have not killed me yet
for writing about your disease!

WHEN THE REVOLUTION IS NEAR AT HAND

We come like a procession of dwarfs
to watch the bloody pterodactyl preying on the land
then fly askance like a dream that mirrors our lives
ruled by the butchers with a ventriloquist air
who come to us in the regiment of the Pope.
A ship is moribund piece by piece as it disintegrates
with no one to gather the flotsam for tomorrow
what talons do they so firmly put in the flesh of my people
that they make of my country a ghetto of silence?

without clearing my words in their official halls
I write the brushfire which spreads charges of my revolt
and dodge at night the bloodhounds they put in my tracks
salubrious politicians keeping guard over the heart of my country
these mad panjandrums in control of stalwart thugs
brandishing guns at the ears of my people
immobilizing themselves until they swallow the brushfire
but never understanding me, never understanding me

thus do I deceive them listening with my mortal soul
until these bombs in my heart detonate themselves
echoing the ghosts of the generation demanding at the eclipse
why they sacrificed the bones in that graveyard which has teeth
spraying their mummies with blood
without their knowing my volatile madness
            *
but when this stream in my head dries up
stretching taut like a huge boa gliding over the maternal blade
a head not scornful but implacable nonetheless
which tossed the first man over the cliff
enveloping him in flames
let this be my testimony to my death
that here in this ghetto of silence there are many
who tergiversate for the blood of black flesh
and like a volcano I spit out my disgust
looking down at Sierra Leone!

THESE WORDS OF OUR INFINITE SADNESS

I own up to you now, my fear of life
indescribable terror scathing my heights
my eyes no longer lead me my name no longer names me
for today a dirty notch hangs from my throat
journeying through the channels of the soul
where no one has heard me demanding of my country
why I starve so much especially today
crackling my knuckles to free my blood body lice
understanding broadly that I exist for you man of the llama
burdened with what destiny lining the walls of your eyes

sweet talk they make of it, this hour of their political power
presaging their absence when I enter between their fingers
gravely registering my poetic DDT
barbaric and stupid then, I dress these politicians
tremendous their monolithic splendour
but for you who ape my conscience daily sweating
suffering from life soul of my soul
remembering as you suffer the pangs producing
these words I write for you now and for always
know that when I sing you I close you in perennial sadness
that you and I understand
      *
that my blood is filthy, dirty faeces of the lizard
that they offer one dinar for my lewd Sierra Leonean head
my lips no longer feel the thunder of our land
but why the hurricane why the furnace
lighting the dry corners of our hearts

of course it is all right that you put your wrong foot
forward when you are sad that your infinite balance
sheet registers nil on your agricultural coin machine
that you give to their riches more than you take

62

from their gold. In short, valetudinarian they invalid
you playing jigsaw puzzle with your life

     *

however, brother, when death becomes our very selves
when the sons depart from their mothers – pain!
and they bring out the rum bottles grandfathers
of our squalor like the god of my soul
who has delivered me to St Phillip scimitar and saracens
where my mother did not promise me life
you will say I was the half brother of the black-jew
my soul is open to the sun.

BEGGARS

And taking account of your malice
your malice to hate without being haters
owing that you starve from head enlarging your sores
by decrees signed with the ink of your pain
and for the convenience of the Lebanese
they turn their water-hoses on you
a monopoly of diseases announce the trademark
of your life thanks to the lack of drugs
and the proliferation of ministers and mistresses
squandering half of the national budget
they build hotels and chalets in Las Palmas
without bothering to learn the language
not to mention the diplomatic bags
whisk through the customs like contagious cannibals
but you limping shadows under the crockets of the palace
starved in your saliva in your thorax
stretched like shadows lost in the desert's maw
coriaceous from wandering in Oedipian rage
how free you are the albatross in mid-flight
recording their collapse while your blood
inflames the burning charcoals of their hearts!

SOUL, CHILBLAINS AND SCAPULAS

I assume a desperate posture this morning
fluteman of the chamois hiding behind tombs
like that I hear voices thin as muslin
bones clumsy as oxen smelling of bacteria
smelling of woodworms and the lingering odour of asafetida

– not a bit sourer than the phlegm from my flaming nose!–

when my flagellated cells dry up
I smoke my pipe and rise
labouring above my pestilential years
that way I exercise myself panting and coughing
from the bloodclots in my head
that smother when the harmattan strikes me joyfully in the heart
in coughing I weep my savannah life and cherish at night
the scarlet capsules of my mosquito body!

partly I practise the art of poetry
because all my country's misery rises up from my belly
like chilblains nourishing on children and it is here
that my poetry assumes its murderous intensity
because while remaining quiet I have observed the politicians
parcelling out pieces of my country
skinned from the scapulas of my country's peasants
my country's fleshy ribs
that broke between their rapacious hold

convulsively when I protest my coyote voice
fills the night from my epileptic being
and racing through the cemetery
the dead plunder me
but it is for you that I grieve so much
country of my soul!

historically I revolt because the chronicles
say 1462 they discovered my country
without learning from the gibbons the name of my people
and tell me what woman will remake my country
sweating from the labour of my loins

I was the beginning of my country
the filth of my country the greediness of my country
and behold the blood which flows from my head

I the admiture of slavery and agony!

POET AMONG THOSE WHO ARE
ALSO POETS

I drive round the dirty streets of Freetown
and observe a man standing at the corner of the library
stabbing his heart with a knife
another spits into the fountain his cola-nut checked hunger
another is crouching half dying under a giant cotton tree
shrieking another with a stream of saliva showering his face
hangs on to the gold-plated gates of the presidential palace
and further down a beggar goes by shouting he has been robbed
all in one hour all in one hour

one woman is screaming raped by a bureaucrat
a childless harlot is beaten by another with kids
at the cemetery three women examine their lost treasures in
bones
three sons like father son and holy ghost
down at the shanty they have turned off the water
because the women have ruined the toilets
and finally a woman has come confessed to selling her daughter

one child whips the other because she called him a dirty name
another is driven to school in a limousine unmarked
while the classmates walk on all ten
at the hospital the wards are in commotion because two children
have been bitten by dogs over at the garbage dump
such is the life seen driving round Freetown.

LETTER TO A TORMENTED PLAYWRIGHT

For Yulisa Amadu Maddy

Amadu I live alone inside four walls of books
some I have read others will grow cobwebs
or maybe like some old friends and lovers
will fade away with their undiscovered logic

the world that I have seen: New York
where I suffered the suicidal brother
and London where I discovered Hinostroza
Delgado, Ortega, Heraud and the other
Andean poets with a rage very much like ours!

remember Amadu how terrible I said it was
that you were in exile and working
in the Telephone Office in touch with all
the languages of the world but with no world
to call your own; how sad you looked that winter
drinking your life and reading poetry with me
in the damp chilly English coffee shops

    *
remember I said how furious I was
that Vallejo had starved to death in Paris
that Rabearivelo had killed himse.f
suffocated by an imaginary France
and I introduced Neruda and Guillen to you
and how in desperation we sought solace in the house
of John La Rose, that courageous Trinidadian poet

Amadu I am writing to you from the dungeon of my heart
the night brings me my grief and I am passive
waiting for someone to come, a woman
a friend, someone to soothe my dying heart!

now the memory of our lives brings a knife to my poems
our deaths which so burdened the beautiful Martiniquan
you said made you happy, she made you so happy, you a
    tormented playwright
        *
sadness returns, the apparitions of my brothers
and my mother grows old thinking about them
and also seeing so much sadness in me her living and dying son
my mother who wishes me happy, who wants me to relive the son
she lost to poetry like a husband a wife to a trusted friend

but already the walls are closing around me
the rain has stopped and once again I am alone
waiting for them, the politicians of our country to come for me
to silence my right to shouting poetry loud in the parks
but who can shut up the rage the melodrama of being Sierra
    Leone
the farce of seeing their pictures daily in the papers
the knowledge of how though blindfolded and muzzled
something is growing, bloating, voluptuous and not despairing
I say to you for now, I embrace you brother.

PART II POEMS IN CONVERSATION WITH DEATH

'Escriban lo que quieran
En el estilo que les parezca mejor
Ha pasado demasiada sangre bajo los puentes
Para seguir creyendo
Que sólo se puede seguir un camino

En poesía se permite todo.

A condición expresa por cierto

De superar la página en blanco.

'Write as you will
In whatever style you like
Too much blood has run under the bridge
To go on believing
That only one road is right.

In poetry everything is permitted

With only this condition, of course:

You have to improve on the blank page.

NICANOR PARRA

'Murio Mi Eternidad Y Estoy Velandola.

Died My Eternity and I Am Waking It.

CÉSAR VALLEJO

THE GRAVEYARD ALSO HAS TEETH

(In memoriam: for Manfred and Theophilous)

Today I have seen a mother's tears today at the cemetery
by the tombstones!
a mother holding the wreaths in her heart
between the ventricles from where a christian God
has fled fixes the stones son to son!
that woman a mother with two stones in her chest
in place of breasts
wails raves and pulls her hair for her sons
waxed in their mummy looks:
that woman is my mother!

Ah my mother
I too have been in agony so long
I do not even remember how to laugh

my mother is weeping today perpetual cothurnus
my mother's pain oppresses her look
I feel her in my soul!
my mother's eyeglasses are in my heart revealing its pus
If I had two souls which one would I give to my mother
If I had two hearts which one would I give to my mother

O my impossible heart!
        *
I touch the wind my mother's marasca voice
not a voice in the air to savour the dead men's souls
not a voice in the leaves with which I paint on my face
the horizontal language of pain
for that woman who does not understand her son
the intense poetry of his soul!
not a voice in his fist but a voice in microwave

singing the shadows of five mummies
sprung from that mother's umbilical cord
my three brothers dead!
my two sisters dead!
to march in death with them
not counting the other deaths in my family stream . . .

now alone which way shall I turn to face the sun
when those who sang the bitter litanies of time
no longer hold for me the key to my life

I think only that I am César Vallejo reborn
at least in my pain!

HAEMORRHAGE

It is this day that I feel . . . heart!
this day of murderous eyes savannah woman
your sons at once living at once dying
breathing each breath of solitude for that same life
which saw them sad tasting their deaths
mother!
I have not known my image blue
I have not known my waters mild
only these gnats which gnaw at my heart

galvanic the day which saw my sorrow
galvanic my penumbra tree to tree
my blood of iguana
my tongue of serpent
galvanic my centuries of delusion!

between water and flame talking to my mother
my mother sits facing the night not seeing her son
who talking in his nightmare wakes suddenly
with the voice of a great river
rising in his head
accompanied by demons!

two demons thus:
come from my invertebrate ancestry
two demons
from my brothers who laugh who laugh Dionysian men
they have not tasted the sun
the way I have tasted it
otherwise they would understand
why I ache so much in my soul
why my name is Syl Cheney-Coker!

PUTREFACTION

Returning home to my country from Spain
on a plane full of Argentines
this perdition which follows me
from sea to sea:
death was in my corridors
death was in my fist in the viscera
in the loud greeting of the grasshoppers' wings
a plethora of deaths
in the myriad silences multiplying the hours

and my father slumped in the hollows of his heart
strikes a phantom of death!
my father feigning life
but already married to a vegetation of deaths

also the other one there. . . Manfred
a man tied to the cruel matron of death
primeval flower lost in early May

ah! to forget that man
animal of the saliva of bitter regrets. . .

I arrived at that hour
dressed in the vestments of the virgin
to cultivate the sea's madness
to remake god and man on the cuneiforms of the tarpon
but death was in my footsteps

brothers I take the cerements of the spirits
to dress myself in them
leaving the twenty-seven bells of the bull
to echo the sizzling of this flame
already flaring up in the jungle of my heart!

PORTRAIT

For George Jackson

> *Yo no me duelo ahora como artista*
> *César Vallejo*

I am this man Syl Cheney-Coker
I have my impossible heart suffering immensely
like the Africans on Robben Island†
from right and left I feel the twin needles of my pain
Africa and America piercing my life
and conjure up hallucinations at night
to make my life nauseous

I will tell you about my life
on the Sierra without a word adrift on the shores
to measure the drowner scorpion of his suicide
and man, man with his impossible heart
nurtured on the grave note of the nightingale's song
in the San Quentin of his day the Folson of his night
on the ebony of his brow
scalded with the plethoric struggle
for my one Soledad for the two sons of my pain
and the dead man who adds the twenty-eight deaths
in his life to the tail-end of my life!

I know that man in the prison of his soul
I know him in the death given him by the terror of his elan!
      *
without wings or legs I go breasting my heart
against the death of George Jackson
that man who suffered my pain!
I see in their lair the marks of their teeth on his body
I see in his blood the men who sing, sing America
led by the Ku Klux Klan

and today without even a stone to mark my grave I die
because in him they lynched me twice
because in me they lynched him twice
throwing his soul to the gila monster

and afterwards man in his death existing in his freedom
exist also that mother with her two sons
exist also the python
exist also America, Hydra swallowing the Blacks

I am this man Syl Cheney-Coker
I have my impossible heart suffering immensely
like the Africans on Robben Island!

† Robben Island: the notorious South African prison.

SEA-SERENADE

I am drawn to the sea at night
as it knots my grief in circular waves
bringing its death-perfumed breath
close to my lips!
on a rock I watch a black crab move nearer by
with eight wobbling legs
under the immense pain of its life
and seeing this crab I feel I am near to my shadows
I understand them smelling their putrid souls!

now facing them pained on this volatile night
I count the thorns sprouting from my heart
for that brother who fled from his mother
on the sphinx's wing!

but in the morning at the cemetery
there will be no flowers no woman
will come to dress his wounds with a kiss
I see already the flight of the innocents
and the blood running down the eyes of the spirits
thrown above the laughing cliffs

ah to depart this comatose life swallowing the fleas
to dodge the passover hand of God
to leave consecrated bread and fasting blood
mother to you that is given the tribulations of Job
indeed! indeed! indeed!
I ask what remains of this catalepsy

only the necrology only the necrology!

THEY HOLD SIEGE AGAINST HUMANITY

For once to go on forgetting my nightmares
the noise and the psychoanalyst and the sad
monologue of the river under the executioner's house

also the mother who defies the violent blows of the cadavers
stoical trenchant double-barrelled grief . . .
for once strolling in the jungle spitting out my lungs
if only to regain my sex for man
who sweats under his universal balls
to earn the ancient bread!

I do not want all this sadness today
now that my soul has travelled so much
in the canal of their insecurity Jewman and Arab
caught in the crossfire of passion
I do not want you fields of Vietnam
Christ in them they make their laboratories
and Moses with his grey beard has thrown the testaments
to the howling guns at night

and after the fertile womb wastes down the nile
from between the thighs I watch
the eleven and sixty-two drops of the apparition
who comes knocking at my door demanding
a father

but when at the musical the concerto
leaves the conductor's eyes and the wandering gypsy
silences her flamenco
and at the cinema they turn off the lights
after showing the Battle of Algiers
and Moshe Dayan sits smoking the hookah seated on
the Arab woman's thighs
give me from their delight a daughter with muscatel lips
for my poet's concupiscence.

THE ROAD TO EXILE THINKING OF VALLEJO

Like others I get drunk in my blood
hiccuping and await the souls of my brothers
perennially on the song composed by the heliotrope heart
at midstream where the spirits walk
undisturbed!
excellent then, this sudden shower of locusts
expanse of cortege and the two roads
of the cemetery where time has its teeth
in the flesh of a mother who oxidizes her soul
with the waters of the passion-flower
as May is a brother just as October was a brother
linked to the prodigal who declares:

Mother I want to return into exile to be your poet!

hearing this, my mother seized by an element of nature
wondering whether I am going or staying seeing the roads
in my eyes, turns a terra-cotta sister and her hair
once black illuminates the night with its premature whiteness

my mother prevents my flight into myself
speaking to me through her silence through the beat of her heart
being that she loves me that she is always herself double
the sword fighting my days the lamp lighting my nights
when my heart sinks deep in the oasis
of its pain! she rejuvenates me calling back the me
that has died tracing the man-child to the poet
without understanding the dictates of my soul
    *
blood absent from my soul my dog-starved days
on the peninsula of my Sierra Leone
my legacies which I counted in five carcasses
dancing drunk in the terrible summers
and that cruel winter polyphonic in verse

when I loved that woman without first learning how to live
I bled one night shedding poems from my heart!

It is recorded then: I'll die in exile!
thinking of my Sierra Leone
this country which has made me a poet
this country which has honoured me
with the two knives of my death passed crisscross
through my heart
so that I can say to a bleeding mother:

Mother I am returning into exile to be your poet!

I RETURN INTO MYSELF

And this is how they will remember me
lowering my coffin my phosphorescent skeletons
in which I came into myself my heart fetishes multiplied
my ubiquitous lice multiplied to go down remembering
the hunger which elongated my throat
the throat which elongated my hunger
within these bright walls of my coffin
to see better the cheeks of a man wailing in his gangrene
with frogs in his throat!

on another plain I could be your clairvoyant brother
watching your steps metallic angle that they gave you
saltpeter brother bitter in my memory!
in another world you came through me seeking Theo
what was that liberal voice demanding that you die
what that parsimonious grave?
you died that afternoon, that afternoon
in New York!

but I, I am tied to the ancient tragedies
brother of Christophe brother of the Creole destiny
sometimes a fandango but never a plantation of my own
or for my brothers black entrepreneurs whose gold
is my flesh made gold by my three deaths

I die of my perdition!
my death of voodoo absolving all the nightmares in my life
for you who have entered my soul body and all
in this river where swims, swims your surgical face
in these rooms where walks your apparition
because to forget you Manfred I must destroy them
insidiously like those who guard the diamond mines
of my country where Africa is disembowelled!

LOOKING FOR THE SPIRIT AT NIGHT

Before my house drinking the peaceful frangipanis
a family of coconut palms shading the nudity of the beach
before my house the termite-infected lemon trees
and the slow movement of the iguana on the iroko tree
it is here that I hear the concerto for death
the wailing cicadas and the howling bats
and the monotonous croaking of the frogs
Sierra Leone with its sad eyes and the medicinal impulse
of a late vulture clearing carcasses off the road
are they brothers of the soul or skeletons of the hour

tonight being Sunday Juba is humid and feeling this heat
I think I'll like to open the antennae of my head
to catch one word one flowering word of hope
before the rain which threatens the night
here where I await the spirit come to live with me
for to be a brother of that spirit . . . Manfred
I write you I call you I make this poem a fountain of your memory
where I drink your delicate fragrance
and then I can walk through open doors
searching for you hoping that your face is no more a shadow
that you are no more bronze than flesh
brother!

but tonight is so peaceful I am drinking my soul
the cicadas the iguana the vulture and the frogs
the termites the beach the gigantic moths
the invading butterflies chased by the geckos
and the matter-of-fact overdose of my deadly solitude!

ORPHAN

Hay un vacío
en mi aire metafísco
que nadie ha de pal par
el claustro de un silencio
que hablō a flor de fuego
César Vallejo

I was visited by Christ and his army of saints
and commanded surrender your soul
to the tree of life lacking fresh growth
in its roots . . .

I am a deserter of your soul
your god-tortured soul
my own will await me fresh growth
springing from the wounds in my life

spirits of water abiding in seashells
a galaxy of mummies beneath which they fix
a bed of bones for my existential self. . .
the word is sacred when I tell you
my soul was made porous following a deluded Christ

I am a deserter of your soul
my own will await me image of fire
image of life I curl in my hands
the orphan of bitter years!

VIATICUM

Edging through self, the man who meditates
traveller in his dreams: his wretched soul
notwithstanding he forges, cultivates life
which is a grenade in his heart.
strange vertebrate of the hour when death is dawning
unfolding in octopus form its adroit self
this man in his nightmare lost poet of Babylon
who dutifully sings his funeral song
and signs in pain the will of his tormented life;
what he has eaten is the flesh of the stone
what he has given is the blood of the tapeworms
to mix with the toxic blood of those who wish him dead

on his horizon a rainbow opens up and reveals
in terror his angel of lust god of the thunderstorm of night.
in vain does he seek his Apollonian world
because his poetry was the saddest of all
and where they await him his place is the most disastrous of all:
Oh to be his mother lamb of the pursuit
man the mule on whose back the whip cracks
to be the skeleton of the vulture's feast
he favours in death what he sorrowed in life
but do you hear him when he cries
with his soul racing through the garrison of death?

THE LONGEST HOUR A MAN LIVES

My brother's long pantomime
demoniacal to say the least
my brother's made proclivity hidden in his olympian shell
in the hour when he is no longer man but a phantom cadaver
my brother's mad proclivity hidden in his olympian shell
and fell the son plundered in an inscrutable god. . .
there are lichens in the hole in which I fell
and felt in degrees my filigreed thorns!

man comes to labour like the brute guanaco
a modern Nebuchadnezzar without the pleasure of a crown
his back to the sun forgetting the pain which tore the woman's
   belly
in her cannibal ecstasy!
see how his luminous god descends and wrenches from his hands
the child of his soul atrophied by his bad blood
see how his hair turns grey scented with the wild perfume
of my burnt cheeks
antediluvian troglodyte bellowing in his pain

alone in his torment man does an ellipsoidal dance
like a demon borne on the branch of the god-tree
in vain does he stretch his oesophagus for the bread of his life
peasant brother linked in common suffering to the Vietnamese
in this his longest hour sanctioned by the church!
but by what does he tell Christ
when his hour is dawning in the necropolis?

POEM TO A GUITARIST

For Desmond Easmon (1946–65)

Death laid its touch
cruel upon your brow
primordial youth drowned in early October
the group gripped
by the savage seizure
of the sea's assault
spun the grey cloak of mourning
Oh the silver chimes of leaving
the silent cavalcade
moving to your marriage with the dead
spades of parting
dug inside the virgin earth
wet with the tears of your clan
you lay cold the early fruit of your tree
snatched by the force of the day
crimson blood gold studded kisses
and the tunes of the several guitars
rest on the soil of your parting
sleep well Tamba.

POEM FOR A GUERRILLA LEADER

To Amilcar Cabral

Solitude supporting solitude on two pergolas
sunset shaping summer where the jungle closes in
man eating roots leaning on the theories of Fanon
it was there in his shadow that I saw the primordium of Africa

slaves supporting treachery behind sweet fraternal looks
minions of the bourgeoisie mingled with serfs
I know it all in serpentine bliss
feeling the tongues of fire obfuscating my life
cheek to cheek with that man in his solitude
murdered in his finest hour
by fratricidal negroes, brothers of lust!

to speak of his name I shed my sorrow
near this sea tormenting my memory with the cargoes of black
    flesh
bought with what portuguese asientos
sacred to the delight of the pope?
Ah when the journey was long sweetening the pain
my destiny to be born a slave enriching these brothers
who eat the flesh of wild boars . . .
my sadness knows it all piercing my heart!

and now the defoliated island rises colourless
the grass is the hands of those maimed by napalm
man-child leaping over the mutilated soul shouting
mother I am going away to be a revolutionary
to remake my brother I heard saying
O island O field you Cape Verde daughter in spoilage.

I HEARD A GOD LAUGH LAST NIGHT

A child talks to me behind closed eyelids
talks to me convulsively like the thunder of hooves
what a bone this child who doesn't say
mother but runs a river of tears between those eyelids
that want to but do not open
how I watch this child in his crib crowned image
of the other one who died after turning eleven one October day
his vexatious form a scandal of surrealism
contorting the contours of his face
he yells, unable to see this blind child
born to a grieving mother I love

there are gods of form the imperfection of malice
like a curse running along hospital corridors at night
like tragedies that plunder our designs
they lurk in catacombs, grow beards and whisper
in drainages, they sit in sad bedrooms with clubfoots
and ridicule the intimacy of lovers
they are the phalanges attacking the ramparts of the soul
they fill oases with terror and cut deep trenches
in the hearts of the pious, they combat the priests of the young
there are reasons to live and reasons to die
but don't we all love today only to be sad tomorrow?

AGONY OF THE LOST POETS

sufro de aqual amigo que murio
y que era como yo buen carpintero
Neruda on Vallejo

From continent to continent the lucid tessitura
the tongues that spoke against the dragons of terror
tongues savouring the primaeval man
between the waters of his desires
from Santiago de Chuco the Indian mother
who bore the last child Cesar Vallejo
wrapped in his Peruvian leaves
and poetry his sad brother
gliding over his piscean soul!

from island to the charnel-house
adumbrating the marginal man
Jean-Joseph Rabearivelo
the little Madagascan exiled in his heart
the starved man whose destiny mother
was to be a poet!
where did the pain begin, where did the passion hit him
the pathetic man, the alcoholic man, the drug man
where did his death begin, the man who siffered Paris
but never seeing it, never seeing it!

that morning waxed in his bones
starved to the knife's edge
they buried César Vallejo
preserving his Andean dignity
that afternoon in his cadaverous shell
they found Rabearivelo dead from a poet's whim
and today I mourn them, the world which killed them
but never their songs
the same world in whose face their verses explode
like a violent brushfire!

THE HUNGER OF THE SUFFERING MAN

Sweating between his fingers, the agricultural man
sweating in his thorax the musician
sweating in his lungs the miner
sweating in his nausea the existential man
sweating in his refugee camp the Palestinian
driven out by the Jew who has forgotten Auschwitz
sweating in his ghetto the blackman
sweating in his carapace the animal-man
sweating when he escapes the innocent man
sweating in their duodena the children
battling the pigs on the garbage dump
sweating the woman whose urgent sex
brings me my brief joy
sweating the poor man whose house starves between the thighs
sweating the deadman, the marginal man
who wants his bones enamelled in gold
sweating the poor who died from the too, too rich
sweating the bronze man who suffers them all
sweating I who sing them!

HE FALLS, THE INVERTEBRATE MAN

And today I drink the riotous water
and rise puffing at each drink between my fragile metacarpus
between these same fingers where on a morning already
   forgotten
the phoenix man escaped striking me hard in my passion
and who is that man who has not lost something
the man without his infinite mother his ubiquitous brothers
the man who said 'pardon me' licking his lice sisters in his blood
the cane man with his immense dignity brother from some
unnamed plantation where the bad blood of his ancestry flows
the damned man strange to the river of his passion
the one who hasn't got a cause like a deluded Christ
without his cross image of my soul

once I howled Africa trumpeting all my sorrow
you were the witness Africa of that plantation madness
you and I dancing to our fallen history
here is the monument to my disgrace the ship hailing my chagrin
and the four centuries of shame like a halo over the head of
   my country

and how the angelic bell rings welcoming you Granville Sharpe
the image of the passage I dare not name each bank of the river
not knowing which storm had plundered them in the night of their
   grief
my luckless voyagers dumped on the spot where no grass
has grown with propitious scions
       *
and who is that man who has not lost a brother
and who is that man not robbed of a cause
the man who does not exit before his phalanges of pain
the man who has not woken up without even his sap to quench his
   thirst
the man who goes and comes from his glacial tomb
It is the invertebrate man behind whose shadow I count my steps!

THE SONG INSIDE THE CHARNEL-HOUSE

You ask me how I exist kneading
the cacophonous beat of my putrid heart
how a man separates the pain from the pleasure
living inseparably as he does from an annual ambience of pain
the pained vertebrate the lost voyager
telling each other about that crepuscular journey
taken one lascivious morning pilloried in my head
you long to live rejoicing in your memory
but suffer inexorably from your germinal soul
tell me from what plantation you take your bad blood

where you go a river awaits you
not long but one you cannot forget
flowing strange from the memory of those who sang drunk
in the charnel-house the tune of my disgrace a memory
of sunken ships here begins the history of my people
the agony of the child who frantically searched
for the radioactive word loose upon the lonely beach
apocalyptic philanthropist of my quest!

to spread bad blood and rape was that their task
I come to the sea where without malice or hate
it is likely that one morning in 1789
the luckless voyagers to the tune of their plantation hearts
made my Sierra Leone the agony of a continent
        *
he sleeps St Phillip my abandoned saint
the convert offers a ciborium of blood
blessed is the blood that is wine for all
blessed be the chalice denied the poor
the man who comes but never returns
orgiastic the hunger that emblazons his eyes

and blessed is the dog that howls in hunger
keeping watch over the fallen man!

but as for me I am at the sole end of my quest
my hands open to the cross of a Christ
whose words confirm my deluded hopes
like this hourglass keeping time with those
whose bad blood draws the water of a river
polluting my country the look of frenzy
of men dancing in the night aping my conscience
euphorically!

DELIRIOUS GOLD, TWIN-HEADED DEATH

Trenches dug at night away from the esplanade
the singing nightingale my own dirge escaped
from lips pouting clouds of rage . . .
mountain of the bleeding country
coruscating with scorn
you look upside down the truncated beast
and give fresh venom to my words

stones circling in waters the innocence of words
sprouting like carrots from the bleeding earth
hills that are loose in the expectancy of doom
and the ventriloquism of men piling disasters
upon the funeral pyres
you were sanguine and now you have drunk
you were hungry and now the slit beast
grows horns inside your throat!

trenches dug at sunset the blood coloured town
we go down Vercingetorix go down like a circus of apes
black gold delirious, twin-headed death
that which they promised us
to live one's life below one's death
to stand on one's own backbone in one's own grave
that which they promised us – never!

we come at morning armoured with truth.

CHEEKBONES, SOB: THE HUNGER THAT EXPIATED THE SOB

Something takes him by the throat decalcifies him
atavistic his sad day of an uncle minus the exiled hour
and the violence of the passion for an odalisque
hermaphrodite woman in whose eyes
the eunuch raises and lowers his dreams
the man who is starved thus and his destiny
to be born in this centruy against whose image
he mirrors his heart demanding
why he has fathered the pain of the child
lost in the sea not searching for the mummified heart
or splitting the bellies of cetaceans
to learn how over the centuries cadaverous man
has swallowed his gangrene but searching all the same

and who has given him this chalice of gold
to drink consecrated wine to the God-carrying
troops of saints, the follower of Chrysostomos
suffering man, minute by minute as you exude
the air of the pain stitched between the lines of your cheeks
that others may read how you suffered the hunger
that expiated the sob the sob that expiated the hunger
          *
shivering, walking diagonally between cadavers
bent over their souls walking boulevards of sob
dreamer of hyperborean days fleeing
days that weep your duodenum on Tuesdays
coriaceous days never slackening up
summer days of septicaemic weeks
winter days of aneurysmal months
armadillan days that close your jejunum in scales
integer the great velocity of the howling days
and the tremor inside your cupboard of sob!

surrealist you weep the litanies of trees
weep drought and desert for the carrion of droughts
weep grotto shut from cold when it rains
weep breaking the scales from so much weight
weep how desperately, pneumonically
tasting the dirty waters from his cheeks
the suffering man enjoys the delirium of death!

NIGHT OF ABSINTHE

My luckless brother feigning a god beyond man
pachyderm life like the great sorrow
of the Jew of Kafka, O tenebrous man!
who listens to that man in his cranium
who talks in his dreams without the Freudian word
pressed, pushed and standing in his skin
so that the primitive of his being resembles
the ductile facetious ape, the superlative dwarf!

shaped in my cyma he whines, curved like Job
lowering his jawbones, the ancient mandibulars
and comes to me through the animal sense
thus do I declaim him, love him, knead him
and fall vertical with him in his slime

to know that life, the night of absinthe
never the sun's coefficient, that piece of cocaine
that will kill the gnats gnawing at his entrails
or the child of his desire to succour him now
beyond the alpha and omega of his dreams
to go on then, like death that grows from the agony
that lacerates life, that kills that dog licking her menstrual wound
he who must deny God to find the sphinx's path
and the river that flows from his tumescent pain

behold that man in vertigo
his diaeresis opposing halves without his syllables
brother I see in your eyes your sundays without psalms
your tuesdays that come without your mondays
and if your cock crows let me see you fall on your Golgotha
for I tell you the pain that grows from my bottle towards you
has no name nor that bottle a colour!

THE CARCASS THAT RESEMBLED THE STONE

Throwing water at the stone of all that is ancient,
it is enough that I have lived in my neighbour's shadow
worn his shoes and walked in his steps behind his death
enough that I have ridden in his procession
dressed with my tears and not in my clothes
now I would like to cancel myself out between the toes
finally to heave in my tracks all my cerebral pangs
the flames of my skeletons where all may dance saying
enough that he lived the sadness stuck in the vertebra

the desire grows from the water grows scarlet and fire
I hold ten capsules dreamer of euphoria hungrily
sapping the blood of dead lovers one September morning
to live off my own worms not cutting deep the blood
of water mermaids and hunger the sister of the drowner
lovesick from the hyacinth that will cure his bad blood
or perhaps the rhythm of a conga drum beating for others
a luminous ray of African sunshine

childhood when the blood was sold to the sea
you who wonder at the suffering man's life
weeping gravely the dog that barked inside his soul
I lost my brother thinking of the pure light to life
his death trickles over my body making me lecherous
as I come to the sea to drink from the silent water

GOING HOME SUFFERING HOW HE CAME SHRIEKING!

Solitude of the water and the silence of the eucalyptus
of the moods man comes seeking that which was stolen
from him by God who like the phoenix salts the pain grown
    enormous
breaking sheets of water like the cancer of life

solitude when the song escapes, the profusion of poetry
dripping bit by bit from his perforated heart
and solitude when the song returns to strip the heart
of so much poetry; corrosive metalloid and bronze
pitiable man like the crab lost from the sea
following death at sunset, a pageant beloved death
O pathetic, terra-cotta man suffering with me!

suffering you I burnt my nails inside my cavity of flames
and measured to perfection the timber that weighs on my death

how sad the night of your exit, whipping your conscience
for not re-living Job for not bearing the cross of Christ
and the begger who limps beside your shadow a collection of
    bones
of Vallejo in whose coffin my own shadow breathes

        *

the tragedy of not knowing when man comes into the world
the tragedy of not knowing when man exits between the groins
his lamentable sobs, his disastrous appetite for love
the pain of carrying his backbone like a monument to God
the pain of all he suffered drinking and will suffer
for Christ at the eucharist and finally falling inside the grave

I am going to close my tremendous chest of scales
brother, close my enormous heart of grill and then
exit, suffering the way I came shrieking at dawn!

THE ABSENCE THAT STRIKES
THE MAN DOWN

Struck by your shadow your great plethoric life
struck in vertigo and struck standing beside your soul
struck being so much of your peripatetic self
and likewise struck when you pass with no one calling you
and finally struck from wanting to be perpendicular to your death

political man when I return to greet you in your grave
on the tiptoes so that you do not hear me
writer filling your prosaic void
wearing your garment of fire like a blade
sealed to the chest you who are alive
confessed by your enormous throat said in your handkerchief
by your great torso stretched alongside the infinite
a summary of thirty-five years and nothing more!

I am going to stay here listening to your groins
to egrets feeding on the worms that come off your corpse
to nails sliding down inside your paws
the great volcano of your heart and the magic
of your image inching harshly to us all
mother son brothers sister rolled up your contagion
a summary of flying bones struck by your absence!

ON THE DEATH OF PABLO NERUDA

Your death has come to me over five thousand miles
while I was still mourning Salvador Allende
for whom you stepped down to present a united front
against fascism and for the defence of the republic
and the growth of an impure poetry (as you once said)

Pablo America did not swallow you nor the generals
who hunted you like guanaco over the Andes and across borders
while miners and peasants kept you underground sharing
their torn ponchos and bread and the fever exuding
the nitrate and copper exploited over the centuries
how generously you sang them in the *Canto General*
the misery of a continent and people parcelled out
like loaves by the generals and colonialists who dreamed
of their banana republics peopled by serfs

and they hounded you in Spain, in Argentina
they hounded you in Brazil and North America
with its chilling hypocrisy closed its doors
to you while proclaiming freedom in the world
they shut you out they shut a poet out!
        *
I remember you fleeing on horseback
over cathedrals, minarets and the battalions of Spain
to the call of your destiny I remember
the ballads of the widows and the scent
of ceremonial virgins drinking your poetry
the only wine they had I remember your sad cancerian eyes
and the lover killing himself because your poetry
had become his lost sweetheart
I remember the hunger inside the incest-infested barrios
and the death crawling like a priest inside the taverns

I remember your great arms wrapped round the agony
of the poets who opposed Franco who opposed humanity in
    Spain

now you lie breathing like a permanence of parnassian gods
on the Isla Negra the flat-footed gulls
have come to sing you the immemorial dirge
and the condors always carniverous like the capitalists
who dream of nubile virgins and stock exchange
have stayed away from the carrion at night
and the iguana is listening in his twilight
listening and watching dressed in your sombre verse
the great anaconda fearless and sad like your continent
unfolds slowly colouring the muddy river
with the umbrage of Sinchi Roca
and the fiery puma struck by the arrow of your death
has carried your message of flames to Hernandez
Garcia Lorca and your great friend Cesar Vallejo
        *
I see Ruben Dario building the ruins of Nicaragua
as a monument to your immortal light
I see Cesar Vallejo among the stones of Macchu Picchu
awaiting you to wrap your icy heart inside his Indian sadness
and others like myself little accomplished craftsmen
scattered like seeds nourished by the sun of your face
mourn you because to have known you Pablo
was life spiced with cinnamon, wine, jacaranda
mimosak rivers, alpaca, ravines, and love
but above all the verisimilitude of how poetry
remains the purest path to living and suffering life!

LOVE-FLOWER FAREWELL

Today I understand better the power of solitude
counting the empty hours in front of my typewriter
hands folded under my chin
lost in the melancholy of Beethoven
and the chirping of the phosphorescent birds
today is like no other day heavy with pain
when sadness grows and the philosopher
has banished love with all its wounds
how terribly I have loved and the poetry bled by it
why so much poetry if it tastes only like a bitter winter
each page of the manuscript haunting me in retrospect
of May days of sacrificial man or the destitute of the suicide
the poet arrived too late to prevent

I leap through valleys like fish through water
seeking the power of clairaudient Gods
I leaf through books like antlers through forests
headstrong with my resolve to die
at which crossroad then will I put my burden down
at what hour will it come this death which seeks me
arms outstretched like an octopus loving me the way
I have loved others to fruition with the thorns of the game
how the innocent ones have killed me
how the guilty ones have loved me
I see them floating in the gulf of my nightmare
the albatross brings me the word:
'Who has never known love has never known death'
at summer your heart heliotropic to the sun

*

to die of the terror of love sad poetry of my soul
where is the orchestra that will play my funeral symphony
already the sea is waiting lecherous with my fits
mingling the drowner with the filthy algae

nothing remains now but the confession of his putrid soul
imaginary Mary woman to a passionate eunuch
the poet of Christ the innocent who died disgraced
the way they crucified him on the hill of his passion.

DESERT MAN

Evidently they have dressed him up criminally
weighed him up in cannons so that the world hears him
on fasting nights of false monologue when his thorax
thirsts hoarsely from bottles and the desert's milk
evidently he reeks of my drunkenness breathes in my collar
thus his abdomen aches from me from the salt cut from the desert
he whines where they have stabbed him for being man
pained him in armour and since he has remained pained
by bayonets separating him from God
I myself am pained writing him this October night

Mediterranean man drenched in your blood
Nilean man have you lost your serene antiquity
they have bombarded the sacred places of the ancient cities
the dead murmur there absorbing the madness of diplomats
who make of the desert's sand their gold reserves
you suffer Moses and suffer Mohammed, do you deny it
the desert is in your eyes the desert drinks from the wells
of your eyes making you skeletal lost man
carrying your burden like a day riddled with storms
and alone in your cave you smoke your tobacco leaves
with a pang of remembrance of the desert holding so much blood
Arab blood Jewish blood that the tanks have cut
deep inside the heart of the desert this October night.

THEY SENT AMICHAI AND AL-HAKIM TO WAR

On the devastated landscape all is active now
mirages and phantoms migs and Illyusins
uncomfortably married without Rabbi or Imam
the bridal procession leaves a trail of saharan blood
serving napalm for the toast and bombs for the feast
somewhere in Jerusalem Amichai writes a poem
before polishing his gun for the front
does he fight only for his Jewish honour and forgets
the damage wrought by the Jew on the road to Damascus
in the city of waters Tewfik Al-Hakim writes no plays nowadays
manning tanks wrecking the carnage in Sinai
I wish they could talk to each other
the Israeli poet and the Egyptian playwright
under the bloodstained oriflame of Christopher Okigbo
a poet who understands war breathing in his skeletons

In the city of war they are counting the bodies
the generals and the stock exchange brokers
the newspapers make me nauseous with so much details
of gains in planes and losses in human souls
do they really want this war poets who should preserve
the universal purity of the life primeval waters
of fratricidal love joining the divided cities
they do not really want this war Moshe Dayan and Anwar Sadat
so after the funeral songs are dead
who will rebuild the synagogues and mosques
who will comfort the wailing mothers
with what wine to quieten the shrieking widows
somewhere in Cairo Al-Hakim has an answer
somewhere in Jerusalem Amichai has an answer
and I await them refusing to be quiet.

THE ONE THAT RETURNED A SKELETON

Your wretchedness in abundance
does not endure you in hospital
it does not bring the matron weeping in your washbowl
does not bring your goodbye nearer your coming
piercing the cactus carried in bird's wings
poor man they have signed you off stretched
along the waterway without dressing your wounds
your chest weighs heavy you won't deny it from the medals
they gave you winning their wars and losing your sons
now they will bring out your crutches
you will limp to your goodbye beside your soul
they will tell your widow about your courage
knowing that you were only half the man
of the other they sent to the war
only the charity of lachrymose Fridays
endures you to me passing your spot

What a pity you were man enduring life
in fits in the desert's cold in trenches
dug in the sun what a pity man
that you faced Mount Heron on your one side
and suffered Sinai on the other, hit in the middle
what a pity that they call you Isaac in Israel
and Ismael in Cairo the same mother though
the belly of harvest the milk of the desert
what a pity that hearing your goodbye
the other has just fled closing his doors
Ah they just passed with Pablo Casals
after striking his last note in the exile's solitude
there at winter desolate water whose essence
I understand looking at the camel's hump
Ah what a pity that you were man like my heart.

THE DROWNER

For John Berryman

Ah! Seeing his backbone mixing with salt it is clear
that the pain of throwing oneself into the river
burns deeper in one's throat than the desire to live
facing one's neighbour behind sunglasses at evening
certainly, to lose one's father to gunshots
seeing the falling shadow in childhood whose agony
the poet writes in dream songs raving with alchohol
as Henry facing the chill of the Mississippi at winter
I mean the anguish of seeing in one eye and sweating pus
in the other dies in man's heart long before
the courage of suicide was born . . . !

and it does not help remembering how he deceived you
the one who danced sweating from so much life
it does not help telling his wife he loved her
the other who threw himself into the river after saying his goodbye
no it does not help, does not help the man now!
the joy of closing one's heart walks convivially
beside man, lives in his sleeves, grows in his beard
and sends staccato pains through his heart at the musical

Truly, at death the drowned man shall be turned into beast
and likewise the slit beast into man and afterwards
reducing God to man, if a woman had lost a child to suicide
that woman shall weep reduced to a child
and likewise the child shall weep in skeletons
and seeing the worms in the skeletons
man comes out cold as ashes with which I close my one eye
the other I keep open to see at my own funeral!

I STEP OUT OF MY SHADOW

God I am happy today truly stepping over the deathline!
I do not bleed for Manfred do not bleed for Theo
in this heart given to pain, today I rejoice seeing
the bougainvillaea blossoming in the sun
delirious breasts of summer maidens!
I want only to live today throwing away my deathmask
that and my shadow which limps alongside the crucified
I tell you feeling you inside my heart
you who are always absent from me like a loved woman
piercing my memory but never saying Syl!

what is this day without the thorns of your son
Mohammedan day or Christian day or is it a Jewish day
or perhaps all three put together a radiance of hyperborean day
the name of this day is unknown to me
brother sister you who have conceived it
drinking muscatel during the lantern parade
what is the name of this day that has caught me gently
 like a gypsy woman holding my head

now we face each other this day of a voluptuous woman and I
eyelashes of the sun drinking rum without soiling the soil!

today I am going to the sea across from my house
leaving my poetry behind, for once to be man
with you God, your son like the others
sombre at birth but who like the crucified
loves despite the pain of the cross
despite those bishops who gloatingly will deny him
for the flesh of the widow and remembering that
I wonder how long this day will last?

POEM FOR A LOST LOVER

To Merle Alexander

Eyes of heavenly essence, O breasts of the purity of breasts
Russian sapphire of the blue of eyes
O wine that mellows like the plenitude of Bach
Sargassian sea that is the calm of your heart
the patience of you loving my fragile soul
the courage of you moulding my moody words
I love you woman gentle in my memory!

O woman of the thirst of Siddhartha's love
you that I lost in the opium of my youth
have you fallen among the rocks off the New England coast
or now in premature grey nurse a stubborn tear
at the window watching winter's snow-coated leaves
here the tropical blossom of an African November
breathes gently on the tree of my heart
Oh that you could have known it woman of the sexual waters
heart of the spirit born of that love
dressing continents with garlands for whom I say
night strike my heart with the purest verse!

SALOME

For Anna Mangahas

Strolling among the eucalyptus, my joy evanescent
like autumn flowers in the wind
and absinthe the pure taste of my rum drunk for the woman
to whose belly I clung tremulous there on the islands
while the sea-urchins festooned the thorns of my desire
for her smile of sanpagitas
her kiss of verbena that kills the heart that loves
you who turned love into a mass of putrefaction
you who demand the head of the son of man
on the broken charger of your hands
     *
to feel those hands like claws round my neck
necklaces of my desire, my subterranean pain
and turtledoves mourning the splendid summer we spent
drinking rum and coconut water there on the island
I speak no more of that island of molasses fresh on my lips
when the tidal waves return to the black rocks
strewn along the coast of Masirik menstrual and sad
only the jellyfish breeding in your belly
reminds me of what the sea looks like
     *
troubadour of luckless summer, I love, living with mesmerized
    blood
my soul atrophied by the sea that turned back
the coelacinth coming back without that ancient pus
in his eyes, shadow whose sadness wears the look
of a man in frenzy upon a lonesome promenade
where others may hear the cacophony of a love
composed in filigree of pain
I who so loved the waterlily
I who so loved the waterlily!
love, sweet, bitter passion
Pushkin's brainless aphrodite the pathway to honour!

Eyelashes flickering my long sadness
that absinthe before and after my song
when I stayed behind for you
suffering the cruelty of your people
their terror that destroyed me, that destroyed me
prisoner of Diliman, never seeing the sun setting over the bay
because the city's blood vampires
wait to suck man's passive frailty
O philosopher! O Spinoza!
man's impotence mastered by fortune
to relive that summer I so wish to forget.

                    *

tonight I'll play our concerto
Brahms' great poem of the equanimity of his soul
but after the Hungarian finale of the violin
I'll lie awake putting out these charcoals in my heart
and will remember forever the violence of your belly
your bad blood that made the pacific red
like the two foetuses you flushed down the toilet!

HIEROGLYPH OF THE NIGHT

At this hour when all seem possible:
a suicide, blasphemy, the passion of the flesh
at this hour lowering my eyes over the funeral poems
which bring back my former sadness
O unctuous delirium!

at this hour taking off my shirt
as if my hour has come
at this hour realizing how I alone
have faced the pestiferous years
sweating inside my heart from sea to sea . . .

hieroglyph of the night hiding inside my coffin
are you the primordial brother or the nemesis of the soul?

I who arrived borne on the sea
the song the ferryman sang bringing in the voyager
a history of bad blood watering the roots of a country
that morning like a plague in the Sierra Leone
of the purity of their eyes that morning beginning the misery
of my people the look the voyager wore disembowelling the
    country
O my land, your sadness, your death!

at this hour remembering how life
has clawed me like a grizzly bear
a memory of spitting out my heart without learning my quest
at this hour I want only to break out of this shell
this day of the volcano of days
and then cleaning my nails, strike one blow at the coffin
to unmask you hieroglyph of the night!

THE WAY THINGS STAND NOW

I draw near you water remembering the harsh summers
summer of Orpheus, summer of the festival of deaths
of my white brother made white by barbiturates
of my black brother made black by the look of my sadness
and my mother who waits at the gates of the cemetery
without flowers because there are no flowers to recall
you Manfred no flowers to sing you Theo!

the night equals my presence dressed in solitude
I cherish my life under the blows of that life
this night I am smoking my pipe as never before
although the water in my head makes it sour
certainly, I tell myself it is over, the road to the cemetery
the teeth of an amazon May like her brother October
and the summer of tall books fiery like shadows

all is over now even the nightmares
like mermaids combing my beard
the hypocritical relatives in mourning
angry because they have been left out in the will
only the blackbird remains who comes in the morning
to wake the splitting torment of my brow.

BEING AT A SACRIFICE TODAY SUNDAY

Suddenly seeing the tomb move this morning
and woman like the pure water on his face
it is likely that he hears her
though he is nothing now but the sun
the shadow of his desert upon her soul
holding in her hand a phial of blood
and a memory of May whipping her conscience
for these atrophied leaves spreading rumours
of the unctuous life she rejuvenates
pouring wine upon the soil of his heart

and man suddenly looks happy in his death
he looks happy sitting on top of his coffin
his shadow will pass here tonight
I read in the blood under the eyelashes

I go leaping over open graves
and feeling breathing the desire that grew
when the other expired between his pronouns
his double atavistic life forever present
where they promised him death silently
in his passion pachyderm in winter

passion when it returns through your soul brother
not holding back the sea in the morning
or the bearded resolve to die heavy in one's boots
that expiated the agony of pleasing God

Now at the appointed time
another African is hounded to death
down in the coalmine in Charlestonville
another African for twenty-five rands
for the Zulu brother of the Xhosa desire
for whom O sea reliving my bitter passion
I am going to wear a new suit tonight
to brighten up my image savouring my death
before polishing my coffin!

THE LAST PRAYER

And who would deny me my death
now that I have tasted it all
the cholera of evening drinking
from the salty water of this sea polluted
by the history of my country?
mingling its heart with the filth of my passion
that river sang behind the bushfire
showing in flames the features of a Christ
whose body bore no signs of his death
to save me as I would have saved him
in spite of my death the taste of the sea's salt
which lured me to him to be deceived by my brothers
as he was deceived breaking his bread

and what am I doing here with this wine in my head
my bitter jaundice to drink for those
who did not serve me at the feast of burnt bread
breaking the diptych to love my brother

ah to celebrate that feast the blood of your heart
possessing only the memory of the betrayed
and not the happiness of your bishops

the bread of your body is burnt
I long for fresh bread to return to you Christ
my death of the cheeks of the savannah
these hands upon my throat
take them away from me ... Christ!

*

I long for the voice of the nightingale
singing in his melancholy
at the hour of my nightmare!
and for these thorns fluttering my conscience

I know already the sounds of my death
registered by boots clattering in my head
bringing out these bloodclots the gifts of leisure
stolen from the fire of the cerement
where all comers at the eclipse of the moonchild
remember the bitter taste of their lives
following a deluded Christ!

THE PRODIGAL SON

To return to you God listening to the cacophony
of this river bringing its pain to my heart
to mix it with the salt of the serpent
lascivious woman whose body makes me lewd
the strength of writing this conversation
with that graveyard which has teeth draws
me near to you God, luxuriant death
promised solace smothering my heart!

the death trickles down my throat
sweetening my candour my violent concupiscence
drinking this rum I drank suffering you in life
eating this bread I ate suffering you in death
the shadows of these brothers whose deathmasks
I wear for the walk to the cerement
what I have promised to the sea is this putrid head
headstrong with my passion here tonight
eating these lice I cracked in my knuckles

thus I smile sneezing into the dust of evening
waiting for the hour of the bird of my soul
I sit alone talking to myself wondering
how I have existed with my torment not fleeing
from this life which weighed me down
thinking how my mother has aged without being my grandmother
and breaking through this voluptuous desire
into the sea's maw I keep time with the mercenary life
knowing that one day a bird without feathers
will come to piss upon a simple stone
beneath which breathes the putrid soul
of the lost poet of babylon!